HOW TO START YOUR OWN BUSINESS?

STEP BY STEP EXPLAINATION

BY DEV

So i dedicate this book to those people who want to start their own business. So First of all Introduction

So my name is Dev i was born on 19 september 2010 and when i was 8 years old then there is a science exmination and after that exmination i was attracted to science and technology and when i was 10 years old i learned coding and maken some apps and when i was 11 then i know about business and stock market and i know how people creates startups but the fact is 98% startups fails in their first 5 years and only 2% succeded so i have also launced a app in playstore and it is going well. So i think i should write a book about how to start a business. In this book you can find some steps to start your business and grow it.

Contents

Prologue *vii*

1. Market Research And Competitive Analysis 1
2. Write Your Business Plan 3
3. Calculate Your Startup Costs 4
4. Establish Business Credit 6
5. Fund Your Business 8
6. Buy An Existing Business Or Franchise 11
7. Pick Your Business Location 16
8. Choose A Business Structure 18
9. Choose Your Business Name 23
10. Register Your Business 26
11. Open A Business Bank Account 29
12. Get Business Insurance 32
13. Manage Your Finances 35
14. Hire And Manage Employees 37
15. Buy Assets And Equipments 40
16. Marketing And Sales 43
17. Strengthen Your Cybersecurity 47
18. Prepare For Emergencies 53
19. Recover From Disasters 55
20. Close Or Sell Your Business 58
21. Hire Employees With Disabilities 62
22. Get More Funding 67
23. Expand To New Locations 69
24. Merge And Aquire Businesses 72
25. Export Products 74

Prologue

Strive not to be a success,but rather to be of value

-Albert Einstein

Have the courage to follow your heart and intuition they somehow know what you truly want to become

-Steve Jobs

The best brains of the Nation may be found in the last benches of the classroom

A.P.J Abdul Kalam

Genius is 1% percent inspiration,99% perspiration

CHAPTER ONE

Market research and competitive analysis

1. Market Research

Before starting your business first research the market. Market Research blends consumer behavior and economic trends. It's crucial to understand your consumer base from the outset. Gather demographic information to better understand opportunities and limitations for gaining customers. This could include population data on age, wealth, family, intrests, or anything else that's relevant to your business.

Then answer the following questions to get a good sense of your market:

- Demand: Is there a desire for your product or service?
- Market Size:How many people would be intested in your offering?
- Economic indicatore:What is the income range and employment rate?
- Location:Where do your customers live and where can your business reach?
- Market saturation:How many similar options are already available to consumers?
- Pricing:What do potential customers pay for these alternatives?

2. Competitive Analysis

Competitive analysis helps you learn from businesses competing for your potential customers. This is key to defining a competitive edge that creates sustainable revenue. your competitive analysis should identify your competition by product line or service and market segment. Asses the following characteristics of the competitive landscape:

- Market Share

- Strengths and weaknesses
- Your window of oppurnity to enter the market
- The importance of your target market to your competitors
- Any barriers that may hinder you as you enter the market
- Indirect or secondary competitorswho may impact your success

Several industries might be competing to serve the same market you're targeting. The Department of justice provides a diagram of porter's five forces as one way you can differentiate your competitive analysis by industry. Important factors to consider include level of competition,threat of new competitors or services ,and the effect of suppliers and customers on price.

CHAPTER TWO

Write your business plan

Business plan help you run your business. A good business plan guides you through each stage of starting and managing your business. You'll use your business plan as a roadmap for how to structure, run,and grow your new business. It's a way to think through the key elements of your business.Business plans can help you get funding or bring on new business partners. Investors want to feel confident they'll see a return on their invesment. Your business plan is the tool you'll use to convince people that working with you -or investing in your company-is a smart choice.

Pick a business plan format that works for you

There's no right or wrong way to write a business plan. What's important is that your plan meets your needs. Most business plans fall into one of two common categories: traditional or lean startup.Traditional business plans are more common, use a standard structure,and encourage you to go into detail in each section. They tend to require more work upfront and can be dozens of pages long. Lean startup business plans are less common but still use a standard structure. They focus on summarizing only the most important points of the key elements of your plan. They can take as little as one hour to make and are typically only one page.

Traditional business plan

This type of plan is very detailed, takes more time to write, and is comprehensive. Lenders and investors commonly request this plan.

Lean startup plan

This type of plan is high-level focus, fast to write, and contains key elements only. Some lenders and investors may ask for more information.

CHAPTER THREE

Calculate your startup costs

The key to a successful business is preparition. Before your business opens its doors, you'll have bills to pay. Understanding your expenses will help you launch successfully.

Calculating startup costs helps you:

- Estimate profits
- Conduct a break-even analysis
- Secure loans
- Attract investors
- Save money with tax deductions

<u>Identify your startup costs</u>

Most business fall into one of three categories: brick-and-mortar businesses, online businesses and service providers. you'll face different startup expenses depending on your business type.

<u>Estimate how much your expenses will cost</u>

Once you have your list of expenses ,you can estimate how much they'll actualy cost. This process will be different for each expenses you have. Some expenses will have well-defined costs --permits and licenses tend to have clear,published costs. You might have to estimate other costs that are less certain, like employee salaries. Look online and talk directly to mentors, vendors, and service providers to see what similar companies pay for expenses.

<u>Add up your expenses for a full financial picture</u>

Once you've identified your bussiness expenses and how much they'll cost, you should organize your expenses into one-time expenses and montly expenses.One-time expenses are the initial costs needed to start the business. Bying major equiment, hiring a logo designer, and paying for permits,licenses, and fees are generally considered as one-time expenses. Montly exxpenses typically includes things like salaries,rent, and utility bills. You'll want to count at least one year of montly expenses, by counting five years is ideal.

CHAPTER FOUR

Establish business credit

As you work to understand your startup costs and expenses, you'll also want to make sure your credit is in good stead. Poor credit history is one of the main reasons why loan applications for small bisinesses are often declined . Poor credit history can also impact insurance rates and the attractiveness of your bisiness to potential parteners, suppliers, and vendors. That's why cultivating and maintaning good credit scores- for both your personal and business lines of credit -is so important.

Maintain good personal and business credit history

Existing businesses have the advantage of an established financial history. But loan eligibility for a new business is typically based on its owner's personal credit score. While not every small business owner has good credit, some may in the first stages of establishing credit.

Apply for business credit

Establishing and managing business credit can help your company secure financing when you need it and with better terms. It can also help you negotiate supply agreements and protect against business identity theft. One of the first steps you'll want to take is to register for a Dun & Bradstreet number , or DUNS number. A DUNS number is a unique nine-digit identification number for each physical location of your business. Dun & Bradstreet also offers guidance on how to build business credit . Before you shop for a loan or line of credit, learn how the law protects against discrimination .

Check and monitor your credit

It's important to monitor both your personal and business credit reports, especially if you beleive you have been the subject of identy theft.

- To monitor your personal credit, visit the annual credit report website, the only authorized source for the free reports guaranteed by law.

- To monitor your business credit, you can get a copy of your company's report from Experian,

CHAPTER FIVE

Fund your business

It costs money to start a business. Funding your business is one of the first-- and most important-- financial choices most business owners make. How you choose to fund your business could affect how you structure and run your business.

Determine how much funding you'll need

Every business has different needs, and no financial solution is one-size-fits-all. Your personal financial situation and vision for your business will shape the financial future of your business.

1. Fund your business yourself with self-funding

Otherwise known as bootstrapping , self-funding lets leverage your own financial resources to support your business. Self-funding can come in the form of turning to family and friends for capital, using your savings account, or even tapping into your 401(k). With self-funding , you retain complete control over the business, but you also take on all the risk yourself. Be careful not to spend more than you can afford, and be especially careful if you choose to tap into retirement accounts early. You might face expensive fees or penalties, or damage your ablity to retire on time- so you should check with your plan's administrator and a personal financial advisor first.

2. Get venture capital from investors

Investors can give you funding to start your business in the form of venture capital invesments. Venture capital is normally offered in exchange for an ownership share and active role in the company. Venture capital differs from traditional financing in a number of important ways: Venture capital typically:

- Focuses high-growth companies
- Invests capital in return for equility, rather than debt(it's not a loan)
- Takes higher risks in exchange for potential higher returns

- Has a longer invesment horizon than traditional financing

Almost all venture capitalists will, at a minimum, want a seat on the board of directore. So be prepared to give up some portion of both control and ownership of your company in exchange for funding.

How to get venture capital funding

There's no guranteed way to get venture capital, but the process generally follows a standard order of basic steps.

1. **Find an investor**

Look for an individual investors-- sometimes called "angel investors"-- or venture capital firms. Be sure to do enough background research to know if the investor is reputable and has experience working with startup companies .

2. **Share your business plan**

The investor will review your business plan to make sure it meets their investing criteria. Most investment funds concentrate on an industry, geographical area, or stage of business developement.

3. **Go through due diligence review**

The investors will look at your company's management team, market,products and services , corporate governance documents, and financial statements.

4. **Work out the terms**

If they want to invest, the next step is to agree on a term sheet that describs the terms and conditions for the fund to make an investment.

5. **Investment**

Once you agree on a term sheet, you can get the investment! Once a venture fund has invested , it becomes actively involved in the company. Venture funds normally come in "rounds". As the company meets milestones , further rounds of financing are made available , with adjustments in price as the company executes its plan.

Use crowdfunding to fund your business

Crowdfunding raises funds for a business from a large number of people, called crowdfunders. Crowdfunders aren't techinically investors, because they don't receive a share of ownership in the business and don't expect a financial return on their money. Instead, Crowdfunders expect to get a "gift" from your company as thanks for their contrubtion. Often, that gift is the product you plan to sell or other special perks, like meeting the business owner or getting their name in the credits. This makes crowdfunding a popular option for people who want to produce creative works (like a documentary) , or a physical product (like a high-tech cooler). Crowdfunding is also popular because it's very low risk for business ownwrs. Not only do you get to retain full control of your company, but if your plan fails, you're typically under no obligation to repay your crowdfunders . Every crowdfunding platform is different, so make sure to read the fine print and understand your full financial and legal obligations.

Get a small business loan

If you want to retain complete control of your business, but don't have enough funds to start, consider a small business loan.

To increase your chances of securing a loan, you should have a business plan,expense sheet, and financial projections for the next five years. These tools will give you an idea of how much you'll need to ask for, and will help the bank know they're making a smart choice by giving you a loan.

Once you have your materials ready, contact banks and credit unions to request a loan. You'll want to compare offers to get the best possible terms for your loan.

CHAPTER SIX

Buy an existing business or franchise

Starting a business from scratch can be challenging. Franchising or buying an existing business can simply the initial planning process.

Know the difference between franchising and buying a business

Before you decide if one of these options is right for you, make sure you know the basics of franchising and buying an existing business. The main difference between franchising and buying an existing business is the level of control you'll have your own business.

Franchising gives you more guidance but less control

A franchise is a business model where one business owner (the "franchisor") sells the rights to their business logo,name, and model to an independent entrepreneur (the 'franchisee"). Restaurants, hotels, and service-oriented business are commonly franchised.

Two common forms of franchising are:

- **Product/trade name franchising:**

The franchisor owns the right to the name or trademark of a business, and sells the right to use that name and trademark to a franchisee. This style of franchising normally focuses on supply chain manegment. Typically, products are manufactured or supplied by the franchisor and delivered to the franchisee to sell.

- **Business format franchising:**

The franchisor and franchisee have an ongoing relationship. This style of franchising normaly focuses on full-spectrum business magement.

Typically, the franchisor offers services like site selection, traning, product supply, marketing plans, and even help getting funding.

When you buy a franchise, you get the right to use the name, logo, and products of a larger brand. You'll also get to benefit from brand recogination, promotions, and marketing. But, it also means you have to follow rules from the larger brand how you run your business.

Byuing an existing business giives you more control but less guidance

Buying an existing business is exactly what it sounds like. The buyer typically takes over full ownership of the business. The largest advantage is having an existing blueprint that can include important factors like an established customer base, defined operating expenses, and fully trained employees. Regardless of business type, almost any kind of business could be bought or sold. When you buy an existing business, you typically get complete control over its direction. However, with no set vision, infrastructure, or external guidance, your business could struggle as you figure out the best way to run things.

Consider three factors before franchising or buying a business

Though the business models differ, there are three common steps to take that will help you determine whether you should franchise or buy a business.

- **Quantify your investment:**

Review your financial landscape and decide how much you're willing to spend to purchase- and ultimately manage- the business. This will help you determine what type of businesses or brands are best for your budget.

- **Consider your talents and lifestyle:**

Be honest about your skills and experience, as they can help you eliminate unrealistic business ventures. For example, if you prefer hands-on assistance, then franchising might be best for you. On the contrary, if you're an experienced business owner, you may want to consider buying an existing business.

- **Review the full landscape**

Look at the existing infrastructure and make sure you understanfd everything that comes alongwith the purchase. Don't be afraid to ask questions about contract, leases, existing cash flow, and inventory. The more you know, the better equiped you'll be to make a sound decision.

Pick the right franchise or existing business for you

Once you know whether you want to franchise or buy a business, you'll need to evalute each specific oppournity. In short, it boils down to this: do your due diligence.

Your research should help you understand the business from both a financial standpoint and in the overall landscape.

If you're interested in franchising, you shoud explore:

- **Any and all existing reports:**

Now's the time to put your detective hat on. To start, get a Uniform Franchise Offering Circular (UFOC).This form contains vital details about he franchise's legal, financial, and personnel history.

- **Associated rules and regulations:**

Every franchise is different. Confirm that you'll have the right to use the franchise name, trademark, and do business in an area protected from other franchisees. You can also find out if you'll get training and managment help from the franchisor, and be able to use the franchisor's expertise in marketing and advertising.

- **Contracts:**

The contact between the two parties usually benefits the franchisor more than the franchisee. The franchisee generally needs to meet sales quotes and buy equipment, supplies, and inventory. Make sure you understand it all before signing.

If you're interested in buying an existing business, you'll want to look into:

- **Licences and permits:**

You'll need to get any needed licences and permits from the current owner or apply for them yourself. Find out which federal,state, and local permits and licences you'll need to run your business.

- **Zoning requirments:**

Zoning requirements may affect your business. Make sure your business follows all the basic zoning laws in your area.

- **Environmental concerns:**

If you're buying real property along with the business, it's important to check the environmental regulations in the area.

- **The value of the business:**

There are many different methods to determine a fair price for the sale of the business. Here are few:

1. Capitalized earning approach:

This method refears to the return on the investment that the investor expects.

2. Excess earning method:

Like the capitalized earning method, except it seperates return on assets from other earnings.

3. Cash flow method:

This method is typically used to determine how much of a loan the business' cash flow can support.

4. Tangible assets(balance sheet) method:

This method values the business by the tangible assets.

5. Value of specific intangible assets method:

This method compares buying a wanted intangible asset versus creating it.

<u>Get ready to buy your franchise or business</u>

Once you've found a franchise or business to buy, it's important to conduct a thorough, objectvive investigation.

At this stage, you'll probably want professional help. Consider hiring an attorney and an accountant. The tax rules surrounding franchises in particular are often complex. A specialist in franchise law can assist you with evaluating the franchise package and tax considerations. An accountant can help you determine the full costs of purchasing and operating the business, and even help estimate potential profit.

An attorney and an accountant together can help you create and evaluate important documents. Typically that includes the following:

- **Letter of intent**
- **Confidentiality agreement**
- **Contracts and leases**
- **Financial statements**
- **Tax returns**
- Sales aggrement
- Purchase price adjustment

CHAPTER SEVEN

Pick your business location

Your business location determines the taxes, laws, and regulations your business will be subject to. You'll need to make a strategic decision about which state, city, and neighborhood you choose to start your business in.

Research the best place to locate your business

You'll need to register your business, pay taxes, and get licenses and permits in the place you choose to locate your business.

Where you locate your business depends in part on the location of your target market, Business partners, and your personal preferances. In addition, you should consider the costs, benefits, and restrictions of different goverment agencies.

Region-specific business expenses

when you calculate your startup costs, take into account the way different expenses might cost more or less depending on your location.

Costs that can vary significantly by location include standard salaries, minimum wage laws, property values, rental rates, business insurance rates, utilities, and government licences and fees.

Local zoning ordinances

If you buy, rent, build, or plan to work out of a physical property for your business, make sure it conforms to local zoning requirments.

Neighborhoods are generally zoned for either commercial or residential use. Zoning ordiances can restrict or entirely ban specific kinds of businesses from operating in an area.

You might have fewer zoning restrictions if you base your business out of your home, but zoning ordinances can still apply even to home-based businesses.

Zoning laws are typically controlled at the local level, so check with your department of city planning, or similar office, to find out about the zoning laws in your area.

State and local taxes

Consider the tax landscape for the state, country, and city. Income tax, sales tax, property tax, and corporate taxes can vary significantly from place to place.

In fact, some states are well-known for creating tax environments that are very friendly to certain kinds of companies. That's part of a reason why tech startups, financial institutions, and manufacturing tend to concentrate in certain areas of a country.

Visit state and local government websites to find out what the tax landscape for your area looks like.

State and local governments incentives

Some state and local governments offer special tax credits for small businesses. You might also find state-specific small business loans or other financial incentives.

Incentive programs and benefits are often releted to job creation, energy efficiency, urban redevelopment, and technology.

CHAPTER EIGHT

Choose a business structure

The business structure you choose influences everything from day-to-day operations, to taxes and how much of your personal assets are at risk. You should choose a business structure that gives you the right balance of legal protections and benefits.

You business structure affects how much you pay in taxes, your ablity to raise money, the paperwork you need to file, and your personal liablity.You'll need to choose a business structure before you register your business with the state. Most businesses will also need to get a tax id number and file for the appropriate licenses and permits. Choose carefully. While you may convert to a different business structure in the future, there may be restrictions based on your locations. This could also result in tax consequences and unintended dissolution, among other complications. Consulting with business counsellors, attorneys, and accountants can prove helpful.

Review common business structures

Sole proprietorship

A sole proprietorship is easy to form and gives you complete control of your business. You're automatically considered to be a sole proprietorship if you do business activities but don't register as any other kind of business.Sole proprietorships do not produce a separate business entity. This means your business assets and liabilities are not separate from your personal assets and liabilities. You can be held personally liable for the debts and obligations of the business. Sole proprietorship are still able to get a trade name.It can also be hard to raise money because you can't sell stock, and banks are hesitant to lend to sole proprietorships. Sole proprietorships can be a good choice for low-risk businesses and owners who want to test their business idea before forming a more formal business.

Partnership

Partnerships are the simplest structure for two or more people to own a business together. There are two common kinds of partnerships: limited partnerships (LP) and limited liablity partnerships (LLP). Limited partnerships have only one general partner with unlimited liablity, and all other partners have limited liablity. The partners with limited liablity also tend to have limited control over the company, which is documented in a partnership agreement. Profits are passed through to personal tax returns, and the general partner-- the partner without limited liablity-- must also pay self-employment taxes. Limited liablity partnerships are similar to limited partnerships, but gave limited liablity to every owner. An LLP protects each partner from debts against the partnership, they won't be responsible for the actions of other partners. Partnerships can be a good choice for businesses with multiple owners, professional groups (like attorneys), and groups who want to test their business idea before forming a more formal business.

Limited liablity company (LLC)

An LLC lets you take advantage of the benefits of both the corporation and partnership business structures. LLCs protect you from personal liablity in most instances, your personal assets -- like your vehicle, house, and savings accounts-- won't be at risk in case your LLC faces bankruptcy or lawsuits. Profits and losses can get passed through to your personal income without facing corporate taxes. However, members of an LLC are considered self-contributions towards Medicare and Social Security. LLCs can have a limited life in many states. When a member joins or leaves LLC, some states may require the LLC to be dissolved and re-formed with new membership-- unless there's already an agreement in place within the LLC for buying, selling, and transferring ownership. LLCs can be a good choice for medium- or higher- risk businesses, owners with significant personal assets they want protected, and owners who want to pay a lower tax rate then they would with a corporation.

Corporation

C corp

A corporation, sometimes called a C corp, is a legal entity that's separate from its owners. Corporations can make a profit, be taxed, and can be held legally liable. Corporations offer the strongest protection to its owners from personal liablity, but the cost to form a corporation is higher than other structures. Corporations also require more extensive record-keeping, operational process, and reporting. Unlike sole proprietors, partnerships, and LLCs, corporations pay income tax on their profits. In some cases, corporate profits are taxed twice -- first, when the company makes a profit, and again when dividends are paid to shareholders on their personal tax returns. Corporations have a completely independent life seperate from its shareholders. If a shareholder leaves the company or sells his or her shares, the C corp can continue doing business relatively undisturbed. Corporations have an advantage when it comes to raising capital because they can raise funds through the sale of stock, which can also be a benifit in attracting employees. Corporations can be a good choice for medium-or higher-risk businesses, those that need to raise money, and businesses that plan to "go public" or eventually be sold.

S corp

An S corporation, sometimes called an S corp, is a special type of corporation that's designed to avoid the double taxation drawback of regular C corps. S corps allow profits, and some losses, to be passed through directly to owners' personal income without ever being subject to corporate tax rates. Not all states tax S corps equally, but most recognize them the same way the federal government does and tax the shareholders accordingly. Some states tax S corps on profits above a specified limit and other states don't recognize the S corp election at all, simply treating the business as a C corp. S corps must file with the IRS to get S corps status, a different process from registering with their state. There are special limits on S corps. Check the IRS website for eligibility requirements. You'll still have to follow the strict filing and operational processes of a C corp. S corps also have an independent life, just like C corps. If a shareholder leaves the company or sells his or her shares, the S corp can continue doing business relatively undisturbed. S corps can be a good choice for a businesses that would otherwise be a C corp, but meet the criteria to file an S corp.

B corp

A benefit corporations, sometimes called a B corp, is a for-profit corporation recognized by a majority of U.S. states. B corps are different from C corps in purpose, accountablity, and transparency, but aren't different in how they're taxed. B corps are driven by both mission and profit. Shareholders hold the company accountable to produce some sort of public benefit in addition to a financial profit. Some states require B corps to submit annual benefit repots that demonstrate their contribution to the public good. There are several third-party B corp certification services, but none are required for a company to be legally considered a B corp in a state where the legal status is available.

Close corporation

Close corporations resemble B corps but have a less traditional corporate structure. These shed many formalities that typically govern corporations and apply to smaller companies. State rules vary, but shares are usually barred from public trading. Close corporations can be run by a small group of shareholders without a board of directors.

Nonprofit corporation

Nonprofit corporations are organized to do charity, education, religious, literary, or scientific work. Because their work benifits the public, nonprofits can receive tax-exempt status, meaning they don't pay state or federal income taxes on any profits it makes. Nonprofits must file with the IRS to get tax exemption, a different process from registering with their state. Nonprofit corporations need to follow organizational rules very similar to a regular C corp. They also need to follow special rules about what they do with any profits they earn. For example, they can't disturbe profits to members or political compaigns. Nonprofits are often called 501(c)(3) corporations- a referance to the section of the internal Revenue code that is most commonly used to grant tax-exempt status.

Cooperative

A cooperative is a business or organization owned by and operated for the benefit of those using its services. Profits and earnings generated by the cooperative are distributed among the members, also known as user-owners. Typically, an elected board of directors and officers run the cooperative while regular members have voting power to control the direction of the cooperative. Members can become part of the cooperative by purchasing shares, thought the amount of shares they hold does not affect the weight of their vote.

Combine different business structures

Designations like S corp and nonprofit aren't strictly business structures -- they can also be understood as a tax status. It's possible for an LLC to be taxed as a C corp, S corp, or a nonprofit. These arrangements are far less common and can be more diffucult to set up. If you're considering one of these non-standard structures, you should speak with a business counselor or an attorney to help you decide.

Compare business structures

Compare the general traits of these business structures, but remember that ownership rules, liability, taxes, and filing requirements for each business structure can vary by state.

CHAPTER NINE

Choose your business name

You can find the right business name with creativity and market research. Once you've picked your name, you should protect it by registering it with the right agencies.

Register your business name to protect it

You'll want to choose a business name that reflects your brand identity and doesn't clash with the types of goods and services you offer. Once you settle on a name you like, you need to protect it. There are four different ways to register your business name. Each way of registering your name serves a different purpose, and some may be legally required depending on your business structure and location.

- Entity name protects you at a state level.
- Trademark protects you at a federal level.
- Doing business as (DBA) doesn't give legal protection, but it might be legally required.
- Domain name protects your business website address.

Each of these name registrations are legally independant. Most small businesses try to use the same name for each kind of registration, but you're not normally required to.

Four different ways to register your business name

Entity name

An entity name can protect the name of your business at a state level. Depending on your business structure and location, the state may require you to register a legal entity name. Your entity name is how the state identifies your business. Each state may have different rules about what your entity name can be and usage of company suffixes. Most states don't allow you to register a name that's already been registered by someone else, and some states require your entity name to reflect the kind of business it represents. In most cases, your entity name registration protects your business and prevents anyone else in the state from operating under the same entity name. However, there are exceptions pertaining to state and business structure.

Trademark

A trademark can protect the name of your business, goods, and services at a national level. Trademarks prevent others in the same (or similar) industry from using your trademarked names. For example, if you were an electronics company and wanted to call your business Springfield Electronic Accessories and one of your products Screen Cover 5000, trademarking those names would prevent other electronic businesses or similar products from using those same names. Businesses in every state are subject to trademark infringement lawsuits, which can prove costly. That's why you should check your prospective business, product, and service name against the official trademark database.

Doing business as (DBA) name

You might need to register your DBA-- also known as a trade name, fictitious name, or assumed name-- with the state, country, or city your business is located in. Registering your DBA name doesn't provide legal protection by itself but most states require you to register your DBA if you use one. Some business structures require you to use a DBA. Even if you're not required to register a DBA, you might want to anyway. A DBA lets you conduct business under a different identity from your own personal name or your formal business entity name. As an added bonus, getting a DBA and federal tax ID number (EIN) allows you to open a business bank account. Multiple businesses can go by the same DBA in one state, so you're less restricted in what you can choose. There's also more leeway in the clarity of business function. For example, a small business owner could use springfield electronic accessories for their entity name but use techbuddy for their DBA. Just remember that trademark infringement laws will still apply. Determine your DBA requirements based on your specific location. Requirements vary by business structure as well as by state, country, and municipality, so check with local government offices and websites.

Domain name

If you want an online presence for your business, start by registering a domain name-- also known as your website address, or URL. Once you register your domain name, no one else can use it for as long as you continue to own it. It's a good way to protect your brand presence online. If someone else has already registered the domain you wanted to use, that's okay. Your domain name doesn't actually need to be the same as your legal business name, trademark, or DBA. For example, springfield electronic accessories could register the domain name techbuddyspringfield.com . You'll register your domain name through a registrar service. Consult a directory of accredited registrars to determine which ones are safe to use, and then pick one offers you the best combination of price and customer service. You'll need to renew your domain registration on a regular basis.

CHAPTER TEN

Register your business

Register your business to make it a distinct legal entity. How and where you need to register depends on your business structure and business location.

Find out if you need to register your business

Your location and business structure determine how you'll need to register your business. Determine those factors first, and registration becomes very straightforward. For most small businesses, registering your business is as simple as registering your business name with state and local governments. In some cases, you don,t need to register at all. If you conduct business as yourself using your legal name, you won't need to register anywhere. But remember, if you don't register your business, you could miss out on personal liability protection, legal benefits, and tax benefits.

Register with state agencies

If your business is a limited liability company (LLC), corporation, partnership, or nonprofit corporation, you,ll probably need to register with any state where you conduct business activities. Typically you're considered to be conducting business activities in a state when:

- Your business has a physical presence in the state.
- You often have in-person meetings with clients in the state.
- A significant portion of your company's revenue comes from the state.
- Any of your employees work in the state.

Some states allow you to register online, and some states make you file paper documents in person or through the mail. Most states require you to register with the Secretary of State's office, a business bureau, or a business agency.

Get a registered agent

If your business is an LLC, corporation, partnership, or nonprofit corporation, you'll need a registered agent in your state before you file. A registered agent receives official papers and legal documents on behalf of your company. The registered agent must be located in the state where you register. Many business owners prefer to use a registered agent service rather than take on this role themselves.

File for foreign qualification

If your LLC, corporation, partnership, or nonprofit corporation conducts business activities in more than one state, you might need to form your business in one state and then file for foreign qualification in other states where your business is active. The state where you form your business will consider your business to be domestic, while every other state will view your business as foreign. Foreign qualification notifies the state that a foreign business is active there. Foreign qualified businesses typically need to pay taxes and annual report fees in both their state of formation and states where they're foreign qualified. To foreign qualify, file a Certificate of Authority with the state. Many states also require a Certificate of Good Standing from your state of formation. Each state charges a filing fee, but the amount varies by state and business structure. Check with state offices to find out foreign qualification requirements and fees.

File state documents and fees

In most cases, the total cost to register your business will be less than $300, but fees vary depending on your state and business structure. The information you'll need typically includes:

- Business name
- Business location
- Ownership, management structure, or directors
- Registered agent information
- Number and value of shares (if you're a corporation)

The documents you need-- and what goes in them-- will vary based on your state and business structure. In addition, some states also require you to register your DBA-- a trade name or a fictitious name-- if you. use one. Check with your state government office to determine what's required in your area.

Register with local agencies

Typically, you don't need to register with country or city governments to actually form your business. If your business is an LLC, corporation, partnership, or nonprofit corporation, you might need to file for licenses and permits from the country or city. Some countries and cities also require you to register your DBA-- a trade name or a fictitious name-- if you use one. Local governments determine registration, licensing, and permitting requirnments, so visit local government websites to find out what you need to do.

Stay up to date with registration requirements

Some states require you to provide reports soon after registration depending on your business structure. You may need to file additional documentation with your state tax board or franchise tax board. These fillings are typically reffered to as initial reports or tax board registration, and most often need to be filled within 30-90 days after you register with the state. Check with your local tax office or franchise tax board, if it applies to you.

CHAPTER ELEVEN

Open a business bank account

Open a business account when you're ready to start accepting or spending money as your business. A business bank account helps you stay legally compliant and protected. It also provides benefits to your customers and employees.

Benefits of business bank accounts

As soon as you start accepting or spending money as your business, you should open a business bank account. Common business accounts include a checking account, savings account, credit card account, and a merchant services account. Merchant services accounts allow you to accept credit and debit card transactions from your customers.

You can open a business bank account once you've gotten your federal EIN.

Most business bank accounts offer perks that don't come with a standard personal bank account.

- Protection. Business banking offers limited personal liability protection by keeping your business funds separate from your personal funds. Merchant services also offer purchase protection for your customers and ensures that their personal information is secure.
- Professionalism. Customers will be able to pay you with credit cards and make checks out to your business instead of directly to you. Plus, you'll be able to authorize employees to handle day-to-day banking tasks on behalf of the business.
- Preparedness. Business banking usually comes with the option for a line of credit for the company. This can be used in the event of an emergency, or if your business needs new equipment.

- Purchasing power. Credit card accounts can help your business make large startup purchases and help establish a credit history for your business.

Find an account with low fees and good benefits

Some business owners open a business account at the same bank they use for their personal accounts. Rates, fees, and options vary from bank to bank, so you should shop around to make sure you find the lowest fees and the best benefits.

Here are things to consider when you're opening a business checking or savings account:

- Introductory offers
- Interest rates for savings and checking
- Interest rates for lines of credit
- Transaction fees
- Early termination fees
- Minimum account balance fees

Here are things to consider when you're opening a merchant services account:

- Discount rate: The percentage charged for every transaction processed
- Transaction fees: The amount charged for every credit card transaction
- Address Verification Service (AVS) fees
- ACH daily batch fees: Fees charged when you settle credit card transactions for that day
- Monthly minimum fees: Fees charged if your business doesn't meet the minimum required transactions

Payment processing companies are an increasingly popular alternative to traditional merchant services accounts. Payment processing companies sometimes provide extra functionality, like accessories that let you use your phone to accept credit card payments. The fee categories that you need to consider will be similar to merchant services account fees. If you find a payment processor that you like, remember that you'll still need to connect it to a business checking account to receive payments.

Get documents you need to open a business bank account

Opening a business bank account is easy once you've picked your bank. Simply go online or to a local branch to begin the process. Here are some of the most common documents banks ask for when you open a business bank account. Some banks may ask for more.

- Employer Identification Number (EIN) (or a Social Security number, if you're a sole proprietorship)
- Your business's formation documents
- Ownership agreements
- Business license

CHAPTER TWELVE

Get business insurance

Business insurance protects you from the unexpected costs of running a business. Accidents, natural disasters, and lawsuits could run you out of business if you're not protected with the right insurance.

Pick the type of business insurance you need

The protections you get from choosing a business structure like a limited liability company (LLC) or a corporation typically only protect your personal property from lawsuits, and even that protection is limited.

Business insurance can fill in the gaps to make sure both your personal assets and your business assets are fully protected from unexpected catastrophes.

In some instances, you might be legally required to purchase certain types of business insurance.

The federal government requires every business with employees to have workers' compensation, unemployment, and disability insurance.

Some states also require additional insurance. Laws requiring insurance vary by state, so visit your state's website to find out the requirements for your business.

Six common types of business insurance

After you purchase insurance that's required by law, you can find insurance to cover any other business risk. As a general rule, you should insure against things you wouldn't be able to pay for on your own.

Speak to insurance agents to find out what kinds of coverage makes sense for your business, and compare terms and prices to find the best deal for you. Here are six common kinds of business insurance to look for:

Insurance type Who it's for What it does

General liability insurance

Any business

This coverage protects against financial loss as the result of bodily injury, property damage, medical expenses, libel, slander, defending lawsuits, and settlement bonds or judgments.

Product liability insurance

Businesses that manufacture, wholesale, distribute, and retail a product

This coverage protects against financial loss as a result of a defective product that causes injury or bodily harm.

Professional liability insurance

Businesses that provide services to customers

This coverage protects against financial loss as a result of malpractice, errors, and negligence.

Commercial property insurance

Businesses with a significant amount of property and physical assets

This coverage protects your business against loss and damage of company property due to a wide variety of events such as fire, smoke, wind and hail storms, civil disobedience and vandalism.

Home-based business insurance

Businesses that are run out of the owner's personal home

Coverage that's added to homeowner's insurance as a rider can offer protection for a small amount of business equipment and liability coverage for third-party injuries.

Business owner's policy

Most small business owners, but especially home-based business owners

A business owner's policy is an insurance package that combines all of the typical coverage options into one bundle. They simplify the insurance buying process and can save you money.

Four steps to buy business insurance

1. Assess your risks. Think about what kind of accidents, natural disasters, or lawsuits could damage your business. For example, if your business is located in a commercial area that is at risk from seasonal events such as fire or hail storms, commercial property insurance will help protect against loss.

2. Find a reputable licensed agent. Commercial insurance agents can help you find policies that match your business needs. They receive commissions from insurance companies when they sell policies, so it's important to find a licensed agent that's interested in your needs as much as his or her own.

3. Shop around. Prices and benefits can vary significantly. You should compare rates, terms, and benefits for insurance offers from several

different agents.

4. Re-assess every year. As your business grows, so do your liabilities. If you have purchased or replaced equipment or expanded operations, you should contact your insurance agent to discuss changes in your business and how they affect your coverage.

CHAPTER THIRTEEN

Manage your finances

Accounting for revenue and expenses can help keep your business running smoothly. Make sure you maintain proper bookkeeping and have a basic knowledge of business finances.

Start with a balance sheet

The balance sheet is the foundation of managing your finances. It operates as a snapshot of your business financials. It helps you keep track of your capital and provide a cash flow projection for future years.

A balance sheet will help you account for costs like employees and supplies. It will also help you track assets, liabilities, and equity. You can get insights by separating and analyzing segments of your business, like comparing online sales to face-to-face sales.

Cost-benefit analysis (CBA)

Looking closely at money-in and money-out helps maintain a sustainable balance between profit and loss. From development and operations to recurring and nonrecurring costs, it's important to categorize expenses in your balance sheet. Then, you can use a cost-benefit analysis, or a process that helps weigh the strengths and weaknesses of a business decision, and put potential recurring benefits and cost reductions in context.

A CBA is a technique for making non-critical choices in a relatively quick and easy way. It simply involves adding money in benefits and money in costs over a specified time period, before subtracting costs from benefits to determine success in terms of dollars. This can come in handy with hiring another employee or an independent contractor.

For example, let's say you're deciding whether to add outdoor seating for your sausage themed restaurant, Haute Dog. You estimate outdoor seating would add $5,000 in extra profit from sales each year. But, the outdoor seating permit costs $1,000 each year, and you'd also have to spend $2,000 to buy outdoor tables and chairs. Your cost-benefit analysis shows that you should add outdoor seating, because the new benefits ($5,000 in new sales) outweigh the new costs ($3,000 in permitting and equipment expenses).

Pick a method of accounting

Businesses often use either the accrual or cash methods of recording purchases. The accrual method puts transactions on the books immediately upon completing the sale. The cash method only records this once payment has been received.

For example, if you make a sale in January and receive the $200 payment in February, an accrual method would allow you to record that on January's books, while the cash method would require that payment to land on February's books.

GAAP

There are many strategies for preparing financial statements for a small business. Generally accepted accounting principles, known as GAAP or "Gap," provides a common a way to standardize financial reporting using the accrual method. Private companies aren't required to follow GAAP.

Get accounting help

You might want to get help with your accounting. Consider hiring a certified public accountant (CPA), bookkeeper, or using an online service.

A CPA will typically cost more than online services, but can normally offer more tailored service for your specific business needs. A bookkeeper can provide basic day-to-day functions at a lower cost, but won't possess the formal accounting education of a CPA.

Ensure that someone can manage the following:

- Accounts receivable
- Accounts payable
- Available cash
- Bank reconciliation
- Payroll

CHAPTER FOURTEEN

Hire and manage employees

Establish a basic payroll structure to help you hire employees. Then, manage employees properly.

Hire and pay employees

Before finding the right person for the job, you'll need to create a plan for paying employees. Follow these steps to set up payroll:

1. Get an Employer Identification Number (EIN)
2. Find out whether you need state or local tax IDs
3. Decide if you want an independent contractor or an employee
4. Ensure new employees return a completed W-4 form
5. Schedule pay periods to coordinate tax withholding for IRS
6. Create a compensation plan for holiday, vacation and leave
7. Choose an in-house or external service for administering payroll
8. Decide who will manage your payroll system
9. Know which records must stay on file and for how long
10. Report payroll taxes as needed on quarterly and annual basis

The IRS maintains the Employer's Tax Guide, which provides guidance on all federal tax filing requirements that could apply to the obligations for your small business. Check with your state tax agency for employer filing stipulations.

File taxes with employees and independent contractors

Distinguishing between employees and independent contractors can impact your bottom line, or your total revenue once expenses have been deducted. Your bottom line ultimately impacts how you withhold taxes and helps you stay legally compliant during tax season. Learn the differences before hiring your first employee.

An independent contractor operates under a separate business name from your company and invoices for the work they've completed. Independent contractors can sometimes qualify as employees in a legal sense. The Equal Employment Opportunity Commission guide breaks things down so you can make a more informed decision.

If your contractor is discovered to meet the legal definition of employee, you may need to pay back taxes and penalties, provide benefits, and reimburse for wages stipulated under the Fair Labor Standards Act.

Plan to offer employee benefits

Healthcare and other benefits play a significant role in hiring and retaining employees. Some employee benefits are required by law, but others are optional.

Required employee benefits

- Social Security taxes: Employers must pay Social Security taxes at the same rate as their employees.
- Workers' Compensation: Required through a commercial carrier, self-insured basis, or state Workers' Compensation Program.
- Disability Insurance: Disability pay is required in California, Hawaii, New Jersey, New York, Rhode Island and Puerto Rico.
- Leave benefits: Most leave benefits are optional outside those stipulated in the Family and Medical Leave Act (FMLA).
- Unemployment insurance: Varies by state, and you may need to register with your state workforce agency.

Optional employee benefits

Your small businesses can offer a complete range of optional benefits to help attract and retain employees. Even if a benefit you offer is optional, it might still have to comply with certain laws if you choose to offer it.

Businesses that offer group health plans must comply with federal laws. You can read more about those laws in the Department of Labor's advisory guide.

Employees can expand coverage through the Affordable Care Act and some may qualify for benefits via the Consolidated Omnibus Budget Reconciliation Act (COBRA). Businesses must extend the option of COBRA benefits to employees who are terminated or laid off.

Retirement plans are a very popular employee benefit. Consider offering an employer-sponsored plan like a 401k or a pension plan. The federal government offers a wide range of resources to aid small business owners in choosing their retirement plan and pension.

Employee incentive program

Employee incentive programs can boost morale and create more draw for open positions. Common incentives include stock options, flex time, wellness programs, corporate memberships, and company events.

If your budget allows, you may want to consider investing in benefits administration software to make your accounting process easier and more efficient. Detailing these benefits in the employee handbook helps your staff make decisions, and they can use it as a reference for workplace requirements.

CHAPTER FIFTEEN

Buy assets and equipments

Your business will need special assets and equipment to succeed. Figure out which assets you need, how to pay for them, and whether you should buy government surplus.

Know the assets and equipments you need

Business assets fall into three broad categories: tangible, intangible, and intellectual property. Depending on the asset type, you'll have to decide whether you want to buy or lease assets for your business. The first step is figuring out which assets will help your business succeed.

Tangible assets

Things like buildings, vehicles, and equipment are used for regular business activity and lose value over time. Things like printer paper, which get used up, typically don't get counted as assets. When managing your finances, you can count tangible assets on your balance sheet as property or equipment.

Intangible assets

Your business reputation, brand, or business partner's influential network are intangible assets or things you can't touch. You don't list these on your balance sheet and it's often difficult or impossible to sell them for cash. But they can still contribute to the overall value of your business.

Intellectual property

A type of intangible asset that includes trademarks, patents, logos, websites, domain names, and software. Intellectual property is often protected by copyright or trademark protection.

Decide to lease or buy

Once you've determined all the assets you need for your business, you can decide how you'd like to acquire them.

Lease

Leasing can be a good option if you need to quickly get a lot of equipment, or if the equipment you need is very expensive. Commercial space can also be leased, so you can rent a place to run your business. In some cases, leasing can actually be less expensive than purchasing with a high-interest loan.

Leasing benefits:

- Needs less cash or credit upfront
- Short-term leases let you test out the equipment
- Maintenance is sometimes included at no extra cost
- Lease payments for business assets are typically tax deductible

Leasing disadvantages:

- The lifetime cost is normally higher than buying
- Replacing it when the lease is up could be expensive
- Depreciation of leased assets typically isn't tax deductible
- Every lease can be structured differently, so look into the details of your offer to make sure you're getting something that works for you.

Confirm the details of lease

There are two general kinds of leases, operating and capital. Since the accounting treatment is different, the kind of lease you use can have a significant impact on your business taxes.

Operating lease

- Works like a traditional rental
- Does not get added to your balance sheet
- Payments are operational expenses
- Low maintenance, risk, or tax obligations

Capital lease

- Works more like a loan
- You own the asset for accounting purposes
- Added to your balance sheet
- Claim depreciation and interest expenses
- Take on all maintenance, risk, and tax obligations

There are other factors to look at, too. Leases sometimes have buyout options that let you fully purchase the asset at the end of the lease. The length of a lease can vary, and shorter leases typically have higher monthly payments. If you want to leave a lease early, you could face steep early-termination penalties.

You might want to ask an attorney to review a lease with you before signing, especially if any of the terms or conditions are unclear.

Buy

Buying equipment can be a good option if you have enough cash or credit available and you're confident you'll be using the assets for a long time.

Buying benefits:

- You can claim depreciation on your taxes
- The lifetime cost to buy is usually less than leasing
- You can count it as an asset on your balance sheet

Buying disadvantages:

- Needs more cash or credit upfront
- Less opportunity to "test out" the asset
- You could be fully liable for maintenance and replacement

Buy with credit or cash

If you buy your assets with cash, you'll own it in full right away. But it also means you'll have less cash available to cover operating expenses. Make sure you've done your accounting homework, and that you can actually afford to pay with cash.

Loans can give you some of the same benefits of leases by distributing the total cost over a longer period. However, you'll pay more in fees and interest than buying outright with cash.

You might be able to leverage lines of credit with your bank, or look for other sources to get more funding for your business.

CHAPTER SIXTEEN

Marketing and sales

Make a marketing plan to persuade consumers to buy your products or services, then decide how you'll accept payment when it's time to make a sale.

Make a marketing plan

Marketing takes time, money, and preparation. One of the best ways to stay on schedule and on budget is to make a marketing plan. It describes the actions you'll take to persuade potential customers to buy your products or services.

Your business plan should contain the central elements of your marketing strategy. Your marketing plan turns your strategy into action.

Use this sections in your marketing plan

Most marketing plans cover these topics. As always, use what works best for your business.

Target market

Describe your audience in detail. Look at the market's size, demographics, unique traits, and trends that relate to demand for your business.

Competetive advantage

Describe what gives your product or service an advantage over the competition. It might be a better product, a lower price, or an excellent customer experience. Sometimes, an environmentally friendly certification or "made in the USA" on your label can be an important factor for customers.

Sales plan

Describe how you'll literally sell your service or product to your customers. List the sales methods you'll use, like retail, wholesale, or your own online store. Explain each step your customer takes once they decide to buy.

Marketing and sales goals

Describe your marketing and sales goals for the next year. Common marketing and sales goals are to increase email subscribers, grow market share, or increase sales by a certain percent.

Marketing action plan

Describe how you'll achieve your marketing and sales goals. List marketing channels you'll use, like online advertising, radio ads, or billboards. Explain your pricing strategy and how you'll use promotions. Talk about the customer support that happens after the sale. The federal government regulates advertising and labeling for a number of consumer products, so make sure your advertising is legally compliant.

Budget

Include a complete breakdown of the costs of your marketing plan. Try to be as accurate as possible. You'll want to keep tracking your costs once you put your plan into action.

Measure and update your plan

Plan to compare your marketing and sales costs to the revenue it generates. You want to make sure you're getting a positive return on investment, or ROI.

Some tactics are hard to measure — like print advertising or word-of-mouth campaigns. Get creative and use others' advice, but be consistent in how you measure the effectiveness of your marketing efforts.

Marketing plans should be maintained on an annual basis, at minimum. Measuring ROI will help you know which part of the plan is working and which part needs to be updated.

Don't forget about operations

Not everyone agrees on the exact distinctions between marketing and sales, but most people recognize they're connected. The influence operations has on marketing and sales is often overlooked.

Simple operations elements like your staff uniform, where your product is made, or the product return process contribute to your customer's experience. That experience shapes how your customers view your company, and can influence whether they'll become a loyal customer for life or tell their friends to stay away.

Choose how you'll accept your payments

The kinds of payments you accept can impact your marketing and sales, as well as your bottom line. Accept forms of payments that are cost effective, secure, and provide a positive experience for your customers.

You'll need a business bank account no matter what kinds of payment you choose.

Credit cards

To accept credit and debit cards, you'll need either a merchant services account with a bank or an account with an independent payment processing company.

You'll pay small processing fees for each credit or debit card transaction, plus costs for setting up any necessary equipment.

Accepting credit and debit cards exposes you to the risk of fraud, but most vendors provide a certain level of protection for your business. Make sure that you use an EMV (Europay, MasterCard, and Visa) chip reader, which will limit both fraud and your liability.

Checks

You only need a business bank account to accept checks.

You'll want to create a policy for accepting checks to help you avoid bad or fraudulent checks. Standard practices include only taking checks from well-known or in-state banks, or requiring checks be only for the exact amount owed. You could also use a third party service to help verify the quality of the check.

If a check bounces, your options to get the final payment will vary depending on your location. Some states require businesses to mail a registered letter and allow a designated waiting period to lapse before further action is taken. To get payment for a bounced check, you could end up in small claims court or using a collection agency.

Cash

Many small businesses operate as "cash only" merchants because it's fast, easy, and inexpensive.

If you accept cash, remember that large sums of cash can add to accounting time and come with an additional security risk. You'll want a secure way to hold your cash, like a register and a safe.

There are special reporting requirements for cash. The IRS requires you to report if your business gets more than $10,000 in cash, or a cash equivalent, from one buyer as a result of a single transaction or two or more related transactions.

Online Payments

If you sell your product or service online, you could accept payment through your website with an online payment service.

Online payment services typically accept credit and debit cards in addition to other popular online money transfer services. You'll pay fees to in order to accept payments online, just like accepting credit cards in a physical location.

Online payment services require a virtual shopping cart to calculate the total, tax, and shipping costs of an order, in addition to collecting customer account and shipping information. Some online payment service providers offer free shopping cart services to businesses.

CHAPTER SEVENTEEN

Strengthen your cybersecurity

Cyberattacks are a concern for small businesses. Learn about cybersecurity threats and how to protect yourself.

Why cybersecurity matters

Cyberattacks cost the U.S. economy billions of dollars a year, and pose a threat for individuals and organizations. Small businesses are especially attractive targets because they have information that cybercriminals (bad actors, foreign governments, etc.) want, and they typically lack the security infrastructure of larger businesses to adequately protect their digital systems for storing, accessing, and disseminating data and information.

Surveys have shown that a majority of small business owners feel their businesses are vulnerable to a cyberattack. Yet many small businesses cannot afford professional IT solutions, have limited time to devote to cybersecurity, and don't know where to begin.

Start by learning about common cybersecurity best practices, understanding common threats, and dedicating resources to address and improve your cybersecurity.

Best practices for preventing cyberattacks

Employees and their work-related communications are a leading cause of data breaches for small businesses because they are direct pathways into your systems. Training employees on basic internet usage best practices can go a long way in preventing cyberattacks.

Other training topics to cover include:

- Spotting phishing emails
- Using good internet browsing practices
- Avoiding suspicious downloads

- Enabling authentication tools (e.g., strong passwords, Multi-Factor Authentication, etc.)
- Protecting sensitive vendor and customer information

Secure your networks

Safeguard your internet connection by encrypting information and using a firewall. If you have a Wi-Fi network, make sure it is secure and hidden. To hide your Wi-Fi network, set up your wireless access point or router so it does not broadcast the network name, known as the Service Set Identifier (SSID). Password-protect access to the router. If you have employees working remotely, use a Virtual Private Network (VPN) to allow them to connect to your network securely from out of the office.

Use antivirus software and keep all software updated

Make sure all of your business's computers are equipped with antivirus software and are updated regularly. Such software can be found online from a variety of different vendors. All software vendors regularly provide patches and updates to their products to correct security problems and improve functionality. It is recommended to configure all software to install updates automatically. In addition to updating antivirus software, it is key to update software associated with operating systems, web browsers, and other applications, as this will help secure your entire infrastructure.

Enable Multi-Factor Authentication

Multi-Factor Authentication (MFA) is a mechanism to verify an individual's identity by requiring them to provide more than just a typical username and password. MFA commonly requires users to provide two or more of the following: something the user knows (password, phrase, PIN), something the user has (physical token, phone), and/or something that physically represents the user (fingerprint, facial recognition). Check with your vendors to see if they offer MFA for your various types of accounts (e.g., financial, accounting, payroll).

Monitor and manage Cloud Service Provider (CSP) accounts

Consider using a CSP to host your organization's information, applications, and collaboration services, especially if you're utilizing a hybrid work structure. Software-as-a-Service (SaaS) providers for email and workplace productivity can help secure data being processed.

Secure, protect, and back up sensitive data

- Secure payment processing - Work with your banks or card processors to ensure you are using the most trusted and validated tools and anti-fraud services. You may also have additional security obligations related to agreements with your bank or payment processor. Isolate payment systems from less secure programs and do not use the same computer to process payments and casually browse the internet.
- Control physical access - Prevent access or the use of business computers by unauthorized individuals. Laptops and mobile devices can be particularly easy targets for theft and can be lost, so lock them up when unattended. Make sure a separate user account is created for each employee and require strong passwords. Administrative privileges should only be given to trusted IT staff and key personnel. Conduct access audits on a regular basis to ensure that former employees have been removed from your systems and have returned all company issued devices.
- Back up your data - Regularly back up data on all of your computers. Forms of critical data include word processing documents, electronic spreadsheets, databases, financial files, human resources files, and accounting files. If possible, institute data backups to cloud storage on a weekly basis.
- Control data access - Frequently audit the data and information you are housing in cloud storage repositories such as Dropbox, Google Drive, Box, and Microsoft Services. Appoint administrators for cloud storage drive and collaboration tools and instruct them to monitor user permissions, giving employees access to only the information they need.

Common threats

As important as it is to include best practices in your cybersecurity strategy, preventative measures can only go so far. Cyberattacks are constantly evolving, and business owners should be aware of the most common types. To learn more about a specific threat, click on the link provided to view a short video or fact sheet.

Malware

Malware (malicious software) is an umbrella term that refers to software intentionally designed to cause damage to a computer, server, or computer network. Malware can include viruses and ransomware.

Viruses

Viruses are harmful programs intended to spread from computers to other connected devices like a disease. Cyber criminals use viruses to gain access to your systems and to cause significant and sometimes unrepairable issues.

Ransomware

Ransomware is a specific type of malware that infects and restricts access to a computer until some sort of ransom is provided. Ransomware will commonly encrypt data on the victim's device and demand money in return for a promise to restore the data. Ransomware exploits unpatched vulnerabilities in software and is usually delivered through phishing emails.

Spyware

Spyware is a form of malware that is designed to gather information from a target, and then send it to another entity without consent. There are types of spyware that are legitimate, legal, and operate for commercial purposes such as advertising data collected by social media platforms, however malicious spyware is used frequently to steal information and send it to other parties.

Phishing

Phishing is a type of cyberattack that uses email or a malicious website to infect your computer or system with malware or to collect sensitive information. Phishing emails appear as though they've been sent from a legitimate organization or known individual. These emails often entice users to click on a link or open an attachment containing malicious code. Be very cautious about opening links from unknown sources. If something seems suspicious from a known source, don't just click on it - ask the source directly if it's legitimate.

Assess your business risk

The first step in improving the cybersecurity of your business is understanding the risk of an attack, and where you can make improvements to safeguard your data and systems.

A cybersecurity risk assessment can identify where a business is vulnerable, and help you create a plan of action, which should include guidance on user training, securing email platforms, and protecting your business's information systems and data.

Planning and assessment tools

There's no substitute for dedicated IT support, whether it's an employee or external consultant, but those resources can be expensive. Here is a list of measures (with specific resources noted) that all businesses can take to improve their cybersecurity.

- Create a cybersecurity plan. The Federal Communications Commission (FCC) offers a cybersecurity planning tool (The Small Biz Cyber Planner 2.0) to help you build a custom strategy and cybersecurity plan based on your unique business needs.
- Conduct a Cyber Resilience Review - DHS partnered with the Computer Emergency Response Team (CERT) Division of Carnegie Mellon University's Software Engineering Institute to create the Cyber Resilience Review (CRR). This is a non-technical assessment to evaluate operational resilience and cybersecurity practices. You can either complete the assessment yourself, or request a facilitated assessment by DHS cybersecurity professionals.
- Conduct vulnerability scans- DHS, through its subagency: Cybersecurity and Infrastructure Security Agency (CISA) also offers free cyber hygiene vulnerability scanning for small businesses. They offer several scanning and testing services to help organizations assess exposure to threats to ultimately help secure systems by addressing known vulnerabilities and adjusting configurations.
- Manage information communication technology (ICT) supply chain risk - Use the ICT Supply Chain Risk Management Toolkit to help shield your business information and communications technology from sophisticated supply chain attacks. Developed by CISA, this toolkit includes strategic messaging, social media, videos, and resources, and is designed to help you raise awareness and reduce the impact of supply chain risks.
- Take advantage of free cybersecurity services and tools - CISA has also compiled a list of free cybersecurity resources including services provided by CISA, widely used open-source tools, and free services offered by private and public sector organizations across the cybersecurity community. Use this living repository of resources to further advance your security capabilities. CISA also provides guidance for small businesses.
- Maintain DoD industry partner compliance (if applicable) - Of special relevance to federal contractors and subcontractors is the Cybersecurity Maturity Model Certification (CMMC) program. Its purpose is to safeguard Controlled Unclassified Information (CUI) that is shared by the DoD. CMMC is a framework and assessor certification program that

provides a model for contractors to meet a set of cybersecurity standards and requirements. It's based on a 3-tiered model (Foundational, Advanced, Expert) that requires companies to implement security measures (and be assessed accordingly), depending on the sensitivity of the information. Rulemaking is currently in progress, but it is essential for contractors to remain up to speed with requirements as a certain CMMC level will be required as a condition of contract award.

CHAPTER EIGHTEEN

Prepare for emergencies

Disasters can take many forms and the financial cost of rebuilding after a disaster can be overwhelming. If you're prepared for emergencies, you'll be in a better position to recover and continue operations should disaster strike.

Be prepared

Step 1: Assess your risk

Every business has unique vulnerabilities and weaknesses. Knowing which disasters are most likely to affect your business can help you to return to operations faster. A back-to-business self-assessment can help you to assess your risks for common hazards such as hurricanes, wildfires, flooding, or even cyberattacks.

Step 2: Create a plan

Your response plan is your roadmap to recovery, so it should be tailored to your business's specific needs and operations. It should address immediate priorities and be easy to access. Checklists and online toolkits are effective resources to help you develop your plan. Consider the following:

- The IRS guide on preparing your business for a disaster
- The Federal Emergency Management Agency (FEMA) emergency preparedness checklist and toolkit

Focus on disasters that pose a realistic risk to your small business. Consult the following resources to lessen the financial impact of disasters and reopen your business quickly.

Step 3: Execute your plan

Practice your plan with your staff so you're ready when a disaster occurs.

Get financial assistance after a disaster

You may be eligible for a low-interest disaster recovery loan through the SBA for damaged and destroyed assets in a declared disaster. These include repair and replacement costs for real estate, personal property, machinery, equipment, inventory, and business assets. Check to see if one of these loans apply .

- Home and Property Disaster loans
- Economic Injury loans
- Military Reservist Economic Injury Disaster loans

Submit your SBA disaster loan as soon as possible, then ask your SBA representative about increasing your physical damage loan for mitigation purposes. There is no cost to apply, and you are under no obligation to accept a loan if approved.

CHAPTER NINETEEN

Recover from disasters

Disasters can happen when you least expect them. Find recovery planning guidance, tips for pivoting your business model, and other small business resiliency resources.

Recovery planning

Planning is one of the most important elements of recovery. Writing and implementing a business continuity plan will help you minimize financial loss when your business faces a disaster. Your business continuity plan should:

- Identify and document critical business functions and processes
- Organize a business continuity team
- Evaluate recovery strategies

Get more help with creating a business continuity plan at Ready.gov.

Pivot your business

As businesses deal with a new reality, and "business as usual" takes on an entirely new meaning, most will need to rethink and retool how they do business in order to survive. Updating your business plan is critical.

If you haven't already updated your business plan, start by taking these three steps:

1. Look for opportunities. Changes in consumer behavior provide opportunities for innovation and new market strategies. Determine how customers' needs and wants may have changed due to the pandemic, and respond accordingly.

2. Streamline operations. Evaluate business operations to find opportunities to work smarter and more cost-efficiently. Review financials, short-term goals, and long-term goals and make appropriate adjustments.

3. Negotiate. This might involve modifying lease agreements, establishing contracts, or future business. Look for ways to streamline costs and reduce overhead.

The Small Business Development Center (SBDC) network has a Business Resiliency Plan Template that you may find useful.

Additional resources

- The SBDC network is the largest SBA-funded Resource Partner and provides one-on-one business advising at no cost to entrepreneurs. SBDC-certified advisers will walk you through your options so you can confidently make tough decisions about the future of your business. Find your nearest SBDC.
- SCORE Small Business Resilience Training can give you the tools to adapt, reopen, and grow successfully through any disaster.

Remote learning

Taking advantage of business training and counseling can empower you with the knowledge you need to recover from any disaster and develop strategies for growth. Here are a few resources to help you get started:

- America's SBDC offers e-learning opportunities tailored to your state.
- Request a business mentor and schedule a remote session through SCORE to access an experienced sounding board who can help you adapt to market changes and develop new business models.
- Increase your knowledge about e-commerce and other topics through courses provided by the Association of Women's Business Centers.
- Create a plan to build crisis resilience and map out ways to improve your short- and long-term cash flow with these crisis-management tools and webinars.

Supply chain

Minimize supply chain interruptions during a disaster and find alternative sources to meet the demands of your customers:

- The Supply Chain Risk Management Toolkit, developed by the DHS Cybersecurity and Infrastructure Agency (CISA), can help you shield your business information and communications technology from supply chain attacks.

- Explore the New Hampshire SBDC's guide to Supply Chain Management During a Downturn.
- The Federal Emergency Management Agency's guide to Supply Chain Resilience may help you understand how local supply chains work together and how to minimize disruptions during an emergency.
- The Virginia SBDC has developed a list of questions to consider when evaluating your supply chain.
- A webinar of tips from the Lynchburg area SBDC may help you with Understanding and Mitigating Supply Chain Risks Remotely.

CHAPTER TWENTY

Close or sell your business

Create a thorough plan to transfer ownership, sell, or close your business. Get qualified advice and know what to do to tie up loose ends.

Close your business

Closing your business can be a difficult choice to make. The Small Business Administration's local assistance finder can connect you with local guidance in planning your exit strategy. It's also helpful to seek advice from your lawyer and a business evaluation expert, along with other business professionals including accountants, bankers, and the IRS.

Follow these steps to closing your business:

1. Decide to close. Sole proprietors can decide on their own, but any type of partnership requires the co-owners to agree. Follow your articles of organization and document with a written agreement.

2. File dissolution documents. Failure to legally dissolve an LLC or corporation with any state you're registered in will expose you to continued taxes and filing requirements. Look up your state for more information from the Secretary of State, Business Bureau, or Business Agency websites.

3. Cancel registrations, permits, licenses, and business names. Protect your finances and reputation by canceling any of these that you no longer need, including your trade name.

4. Comply with employment and labor laws. Reference the Department of Labor's Worker Adjustment and Retraining Notification Act (WARN) for employee payment after closing, along with other federal and state laws.

5. Resolve financial obligations. Handle final returns for income tax and sales tax. Cancel your Employer Identification Number, notify federal and state tax agencies, and follow this checklist from the IRS with instructions on how to close your business.

6. Maintain records. You may be legally required to maintain tax and employment records, among other files. Common guidelines advise keeping

records for anywhere from three to seven years.

Sell your business

After careful consideration, you may decide to sell your business. Sound planning can help ensure you cover all your bases.

Use business valuation to set a monetary value before marketing to prospective buyers. You can do a self-evaluation and learn more about the resources needed for business valuation appraisals from The Appraisal Foundation.

Accurately value all property and real estate tied to your small business. This can include intangible assets like brand presence, intellectual property, customer information, and projection of future revenue.

When you're figuring out how much your business is worth, consider these common valuation methods:

1. Income approach. Looks at projected revenue and accounts for potential risks.
2. Market approach. Compares your business to other similar businesses that have recently sold.
3. Assets approach. Subtracts total business liabilities from the total value of all assets.

Make a sales agreement

You must prepare a sales agreement to sell your business officially. This document allows for the purchase of assets or stock of a corporation. An attorney should review it to make sure it's accurate and comprehensive.

List all inventory in the sale along with names of the seller, buyer, and business. Fill in background details. Determine how the business will be run prior to close and the level of access the buyer will have to your information. Note all adjustments, broker fees, and any other aspects relevant to the terms of agreement.

Don't leave out any assets and liabilities, or this can create problems even after the sale has been finalized.

Transfer your ownership

Many small business owners will face a time when they need to transfer their ownership rights to another person or entity. You'll have a few different options available for doing so.

Option Scenario Benefit

Outright sale

Liz owns a local clothing boutique that hasn't performed well. With several other businesses on her plate, she can no longer afford to continue running it. She needs a quick exit and quick cash.

By selling a business in full, you will transfer ownership immediately and receive payment right away.

Gradual sale

Bill owns a market near his home. After the birth of his granddaughter, he now spends most of his time at his daughter's home several hours away. After transferring business ownership, Bill no longer has to worry about running his business but is still receiving a monthly income.

This option often benefits individuals that can't afford an outright sale, but instead are able to finance a long-term payment plan. A gradual sale is a flexible option for transferring a business.

Lease agreement

Barbara has decided to take a year-long cruise around the world. To take care of her day care center she's decided to transfer ownership to a friend through a lease.

By transferring your business ownership through a lease, you'll commit to a contract that details the conditions and payments you'll receive for the temporary rights to the business.

Other consedirations

Transferring ownership of a family business may have legal impacts, such as estate and gift tax obligations imposed by the IRS. A transfer of property would also likely require taxation.

It's also important to understand how to approach the exit strategy based on business type. You may want to consult with a lawyer to see which additional rules could apply.

File for bankruptcy or liquidate

A forced exit has implications for your employees, assets and tax obligations.

During a bankruptcy case, you need to stay up to date with all filing requirements and taxes. Reference the IRS Bankruptcy Tax Guide online for information on debt cancellation, tax procedures, and considerations for different types of business structures.

Liquidating assets usually comes as a last-resort strategy after no buyers, merges, or successors appear on the horizon. This process of redistributing assets to creditors and shareholders still requires a sound plan of action.

Before terminating your lease, selling equipment, and disconnecting utilities, talk to your lawyer and accountant. They'll help you develop a plan to present to creditors, whose cooperation you need during this process.

Reference these steps in the asset liquidation process.

1. Prepare an inventory and determine assets for sale
2. Secure your merchandise
3. Set liquidation value of assets with a qualified appraiser
4. Use that value to estimate net sale proceeds and re-evaluate your decision
5. Choose sale type: negotiated, consignment, internet, sealed bid, or retail
6. Select the best time and location for your sale
7. Hire an auctioneer, dealer, broker, or other expert to conduct
8. Use a non-recourse bill of sale so buyer accepts the associated risk

CHAPTER TWENTY-ONE

Hire employees with disabilities

Hiring individuals with disabilities can be a smart move for your business.

Now more than ever, small businesses are finding it challenging to hire talented workers. Hiring disabled individuals can help businesses meet their talent needs while strengthening their competitive edge. By hiring individuals with disabilities, businesses can:

Expand their pool of talent

- Create a culture of diversity
- Meet their workforce needs
- Foster creative business solutions

Generate goodwill among customers

A disability is considered a physical or mental impairment that substantially limits one or more major life activity. Individuals with disabilities often need workplace accommodations—a modification or adjustment to a job, the work environment, or the way things are usually done during the hiring process.

Small businesses benefit when they value and appreciate each person for their individual differences and experiences. By investing in recruiting, hiring, and retaining talent—including people with disabilities—businesses can give themselves a competitive edge and demonstrate their commitment to inclusion.

Create a culture of inclusivity

Creating an inclusive culture isn't hard, but it does take some planning and commitment. The following guidelines are a starting point to assist you with common recruiting and workplace issues. For detailed information on creating an inclusive culture, check out the Inclusion@Work framework from the Employer Assistance and Resource Network on Disability Inclusion (EARN). EARN is funded by the U.S. Department of Labor (DOL).

Write an inclusive job posting

The first step in this process is to write a good job description. The job description should be used to delineate tasks, duties, and expectations for both the employer and the employee.

An inclusive job description should define expectations and identify potential accommodations that can enable employees to perform their job successfully and benefit all job seekers. EARN offers a guide to writing an inclusive job description.

Find qualified talent

The goal of the recruitment process is to attract and identify individuals who have the best mix of skills and attributes for the job available. Ensuring that all qualified individuals—including those with disabilities—can take part in the process is essential to achieving this goal. It is important to know where to look to find candidates with disabilities beyond the traditional recruiting processes. Companies interested in hiring employees with disabilities should begin by:

- Reaching out to the local Workforce Development Board (WDB). WDBs are part of the Public Workforce System, a network of federal, state, and local offices that connect companies to the resources they need to strengthen their business and their workforce, including skilled employees with disabilities.
- Connecting with a Business Services Representative at a local American Job Center. They provide assistance with recruiting, hiring or training employees, including people with disabilities who are ready and willing to work.
- EARN offers a list of online job posting boards that can help small businesses find qualified workers with disabilities.

Customize your employee search

Customized employment strategies help small businesses identify low-cost, low-tech methods for improving labor effectiveness and task distribution to assure a mutually rewarding employment partnership. These strategies aid in recruiting workers with disabilities who are well-situated based on their skills, talents, and experiences to meet the specific needs unique to a small business.

The U.S. Department of Labor's Office on Disability Employment Policy has developed significant resources, videos, and research to support employers in implementing customized employment strategies within their recruitment and hiring processes.

Partner with advocacy groups and workforce development organizations

Expand your reach by partnering with groups such as:

- State Vocational Rehabilitation (VR) agencies, who provide a wide range of services to help people with disabilities train for, find, and keep jobs that fit their skills and interests. They can also connect businesses with skilled workers with disabilities in their area. For more information, contact your state VR agency.
- Your state's Governor's Committee on Employment of People with Disabilities. These state offices work to increase employment opportunities for people with disabilities and to promote public awareness of the needs and abilities of people with disabilities.
- Your local Center for Independent Living (CIL). These organizations promote independent living and equal access for people of all ages with all types of disabilities. They often work with local employers interested in hiring qualified workers with disabilities.
- State Apprenticeship Agencies help connect jobseekers looking to learn new skills with employers and sponsors looking for qualified workers. Apprenticeships help develop a workforce that has industry-driven training and give employers a competitive edge. They can also help increase workforce inclusion. Watch the #ApprenticeshipWorks video to learn more about these benefits.
- The Social Security Administration's Ticket to Work (TTW) program can connect employers with Employment Networks that help businesses find qualified job applicants with disabilities.
- A local college or university's Office of Disability Student Services. They may be able to connect you to students with disabilities pursuing various fields of study who are interested in internships or employment opportunities with a business like yours.

Cultivating relationships with these organizations is a good way to gain visibility and will grant you better access to the talent pool of people with disabilities.

Know the guidelines on interviewing

When interviewing candidates with disabilities, employers must follow certain guidelines. For example, there are certain questions you may not ask job applicants regarding their disabilities or medical conditions.

To learn how to conduct such interviews, read the U.S. Equal Employment Opportunity Commission guide, "Questions and Answers: Enforcement Guidance on Disability-Related Inquiries and Medical Examinations of Employees under the Americans with Disabilities Act."

Reasonable job accommodations

What matters is an employee's abilities, not his or her disabilities. Job accommodations help employees with disabilities perform certain tasks that are essential for them to do their job.

The Americans with Disabilities Act (ADA) considers an accommodation to be "any modification or adjustment to a job or work environment that enables a qualified person with a disability to apply for or perform a job."

Job accommodations can include:

- Screen reading software for employees who have low vision,
- Raised desks for employees who use wheelchairs,
- Job coaching for employees with intellectual disabilities,
- Workplace Personal Assistance Services,
- Working from home (telecommuting)
- Adjustments to work schedules.

Cost of accommodations

Most workplace accommodations don't cost much. According to the Job Accommodation Network (JAN), half of all job accommodations cost employers nothing. Of those that do have a cost, the typical one-time expenditure is $500—an expense that most employers say pays for itself many times over through reduced insurance and training costs and increased productivity.

Businesses can take advantage of financial incentives to make reasonable accommodations.

Accessible technology

To participate fully in the workforce, individuals with disabilities must be able to access the same information as individuals without disabilities.

Make your workplace technology and information accessible for all employees and jobseekers by ensuring your online job applications, pre-employment tests, resume upload programs and other recruitment tools are accessible. For additional information about accessible technology:

- Read Accessible Technology Action Steps: A Guide for Employers. Developed by Department of Labor-funded Partnership on Employment & Accessible Technology (PEAT), this guide shows you how to review your workplace technology for accessibility.
- Use PEAT's TechCheck tool to review your technology accessibility practices and find tools to improve them.
- PEAT's TalentWorks tool helps employers and human resources (HR) professionals make their digital recruiting technologies accessible to all job seekers.

CHAPTER TWENTY-TWO

Get more funding

If your business is up and running but needs more capital, you can rely on familiar options. However, funding an existing business still requires slightly different preparation.

Prepare to request more funding

Anyone who gives you funds wants to feel confident that their investment will pay off. Prepare a business case and financial statements to convince lenders, crowdfunders, or investors to fund your small business.

Make your business case

You'll need to make a solid business case for more funding. Produce a short statement with the total requested amount and specific reasons for it.

Maybe your business is cyclical — like construction or education — and could use funding to get through expected slow periods. Or maybe it needs capital to invest in new machinery or launch a product line. Whatever the reason, update your business plan to include this stage of funding.

A business case should give assurances that new funds won't be mismanaged. Include descriptions of your management team to highlight their skills and expertise.

Prepare financial statements

Display that your business is doing well with financial history statements. Show how your business has grown by reporting revenue, expenses, and profit over time. If you don't have a history of positive growth, explain why more funding will allow you turn it around.

Prove you're financially responsible with a business credit report. If you've already applied for a DUNS number, you can get a business credit report from Dun & Bradstreet. Review your business credit file to make sure it's accurate before sharing it.

Determine how much your company is worth today by performing a business valuation. This is the same process you'd go through if you were planning to sell your business. Valuation methods vary, but you can do a self-evaluation or seek out a qualified business appraiser.

Show how your business will grow in the future with a forecast. Your business forecast can be based on intuitive judgement, quantitative analysis, or both. Show your projected revenue and expenses, and clearly explain how you arrived at those estimations.

Choose your funding source

Get loans, credit, or crowdfunding

Additional funding options for existing business are similar to funding options for a new business. You'll have the same general set of options, which include small business loans, credit cards, and crowdfunding.

Existing businesses have the advantage of an established financial history with credit reports, business bank accounts, and internal financial reports. Lenders, investors, and even crowdfunders can use that information when they decide whether to fund your business.

Sell ownership in your company

If you decide to sell an ownership stake of your company, your business structure will determine your options. Remember, whenever you sell ownership in your company, you dilute the ownership of current owners.

An LLC or a partnership can accept new members and give them a percentage of ownership in exchange for a capital investment. Just make sure you comply with your articles of organization and operating or partnership agreements. Then notify your state as necessary. Some states may require your LLC to be dissolved and re-formed with new membership.

Corporations can sell shares of the company, so long as it's done in compliance with your articles of incorporation and bylaws. Again, notify your state if necessary.

CHAPTER TWENTY-THREE

Expand to new locations

Once you're ready to expand, update the marketing plan and confirm that your business is financially prepared. Then, make sure to comply with all laws, rules, and regulations in the new business locations.

Prepare for a new market

First, update your marketing plan with your new location in mind. Think about your target customer, sales plan, and competitive advantage. Add up any additional marketing and sales costs. Make sure your updated marketing plan is just as thorough as your initial plan.

Compare your business to the competition, learn about the local market, and get a sense of the advertising market.

Next, review your business finances. Build a forecast that projects estimated costs and estimated revenue for your new location. Take a close look at your balance sheet to make sure you can cover the costs of expanding. If you don't have enough capital, you can try to get more funding.

Legal steps to expand your business

Expanding your business to a new state, county, or city isn't very different from opening a new business there. You'll want to make sure you register your business with the right agencies and pay the appropriate taxes.

License, permit, and zoning rules

These rules vary across states and localities. Getting licenses and permits in new locations is similar to getting them in your home state.

If you already have a permit or license from a federal agency, check with the issuing agency to confirm you can legally operate in a new state. Also, see whether your new state, county, and city governments require a new license or permit. Start by visiting your state's website.

Foreign qualification

If you plan to expand your business to a new state, you might need to file for foreign qualification in that state. This process notifies the new state that your business is active there.

To foreign qualify, file a Certificate of Authority. Many states also require a Certificate of Good Standing from your state of formation. Each state charges a filing fee, but the amount varies by location and business structure.

Check with state offices to find out foreign qualification requirements and fees.

Pay taxes in new states and localities

If you do business in a new state as a foreign qualified business, you'll typically need to pay taxes and annual report fees in the new state as well as your home state. The process for foreign qualified businesses to pay taxes is similar to any other business that needs to pay taxes in the state.

Keep in mind that not every state and locality has a sales tax. In addition, most states have tax exemptions on certain items, such as food or clothing. If you charge sales tax, you need to be familiar with applicable rates.

Pay taxes for online sales

If your business has a physical presence in a state — such as a store, office, or warehouse — you must collect applicable state and local sales tax from your customers in that state. If you don't have a physical presence in a particular state, you're not required to collect sales taxes.

Determining which sales tax to charge can be a challenge. Many retailers use online shopping cart software that automatically calculates sales tax rates. Make sure your sales plan accounts for the various state rates.

Franchising

There are two primary ways you could expand your business with franchising.

The first way is to buy an existing business or franchise. This option tends to cost more upfront, but can be less risky than trying to start from scratch.

The second way is to build your own franchise. Businesses that are good candidates for franchising have a few traits in common.

- Product or service is superior and appeals to potential business owners
- Concept and operations are easy to teach
- Business is easy to duplicate in new markets

The federal government and many states have requirements that must be met in order for you to sell franchises, so you may want to hire an attorney. Once you've begun franchising, some states remain active in the relationship between you and your franchisees by monitoring territorial rights or limiting the transfer and renewal of your franchises.

Franchising has more costs than many other types of businesses. You'll probably need to pay lawyers, accountants, and advertising staff. Don't forget about training the employees and building systems you'll need to run the franchise.

CHAPTER TWENTY-FOUR

Merge and aquire businesses

You can grow your business by buying or merging with a smaller business. The process is similar to starting a new business, but you need to take extra steps to protect your existing business.

Differences between mergers and acquisitions

Mergers and acquisitions are similar but have a few major differences.

Mergers combine two separate businesses into a single new legal entity. True mergers are uncommon because it's rare for two equal companies to mutually benefit from combining resources and staff, including their CEOs.

Unlike mergers, acquisitions do not result in the formation of a new company. Instead, the purchased company gets fully absorbed by the acquiring company. Sometimes this means the acquired company gets liquidated. Acquiring a business is similar to buying an existing business or franchise.

Calculate how much the other business is worth

Conduct a business valuation to determine the value of the other business before you agree to a sale. This is essentially the same process you'd go through to figure out how much your own business is worth before closing or selling your business.

There are several ways to value a business, so do extensive research on methods if you choose to do it on your own. You might want to hire a qualified business appraiser. Once you know how much the other business is worth, you'll know whether you can afford it outright or if you need to get more funding.

Make a merger or acquisition agreement

You must prepare a sales agreement to move forward with the sale or merger. This document allows for the purchase of assets or stock of a corporation. An attorney should review it to make sure it's accurate and comprehensive.

List all inventory in the sale along with names of the businesses and owners. Fill in the relevant background details. Determine how the business will be run prior to close and the level of access each company will have to financial information. Note all adjustments, broker fees, and any other aspects relevant to the terms of agreement.

Don't leave out any assets and liabilities, or this can create problems even after the sale has been finalized.

Transfer business ownership

The terms of your agreement will dictate which steps you must take to transfer ownership, and what that ownership will look like. It's widely recommended to have an attorney help with this step.

After you've completed the acquisition or merger, you'll need to register these changes with the state, depending on state law and business structure.

CHAPTER TWENTY-FIVE

Export Products

Export goods to increase your profits, reduce market dependence, and stabilize seasonal sales. Connect with SBA resources and partners to get help exporting.

Get export and trade assistance

It may be easier to expand your market than you think. Even small businesses can get into exporting with the help of mentors and modern technology.

Find international buyers

Many small business owners don't realize foreign sales opportunities are well within reach. To reach them, all you need to do is take advantage of federal programs designed to build the bridge to new markets.

www.ingramcontent.com/pod-product-compliance
Ingram Content Group UK Ltd.
Pitfield, Milton Keynes, MK11 3LW, UK
UKHW021924190726
13853UKWH00002B/836